My name is _____, and

I'm _____ years old. This book has been given to

me by _____. I've been asked to

be in the wedding of _____ and

_____, which will take place at

_____ on _____. I know the bride

and groom because_____.

Library of Congress Cataloging-in-Publication Data

Plaisted, Caroline.
I'm in the wedding, too: a complete guide for flower girls and
junior bridesmaids/by Caroline Plaisted; illustrated by Joanna Walsh.
p. cm.
Summary: Describes the events of a typical wedding day and explains
the responsibilities of the various participants with special emphasis
on the role and duties of the flower girl and junior bridesmaid.
ISBN 0-525-45752-6
I. Wedding attendants—Juvenile literature.   2. Wedding etiquette—
Juvenile literature.   [I. Weddings.   2. Wedding etiquette.   3. Etiquette.]
I. Walsh, Joanna, ill.   II. Title.
BJ2065.W43P53   1997   395'.22—dc20
96-9122   CIP   AC

Published in the United States 1997 by Dutton Children's Books,
a division of Penguin Books USA Inc.
375 Hudson Street, New York, New York 10014
Originally published in Great Britain 1996 by
Bloomsbury Publishing PLC, London
Typography by Julia Goodman
Printed in Hong Kong
First American Edition
4 6 8 10 9 7 5

Caroline Plaisted ❧ Joanna Walsh

I'm in the Wedding Too

A Complete Guide for
Flower Girls & Junior
Bridesmaids

DUTTON CHILDREN'S BOOKS

Congratulations

Congratulations! You have been chosen to be one of the special people included in an important occasion—a wedding. Being part of the wedding will be exciting, but there will be many things to do and remember.

This book is for you to read and write in as you prepare for the big day. You will read about all the people who will be at the wedding. And you will learn what you are expected to do and what you should practice so that you'll be ready when the exciting day comes. You can record important details, and there's a place to keep photographs and souvenirs so that you will always remember this special day.

Who Will Be at the Wedding?

Some couples like to have only a few guests at their wedding, while others might invite many people. No matter how big or small the wedding is, these people will definitely be there:

The Bride and Groom

These are the two most important people. Without them, there would be no wedding at all!

The Officiator

In a church, a priest or minister will conduct the wedding ceremony. In a synagogue, there will be a rabbi. For a nonreligious ceremony, a judge or other authorized person will officiate.

The Best Man

Often the groom's best friend or a close relative is invited to help the groom and make sure that everything goes smoothly. At the ceremony, the ring bearer passes him the wedding rings, which he hands to the officiator. At the reception, he will make a special toast to the bride and groom.

At many weddings, you will also find these people:

The Maid or Matron of Honor

She will help the bride on the day of the wedding and will look after all the bride's attendants.

The Bridesmaids & Flower Girls

Other girls and young women who have been chosen by the bride to attend her.

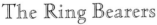

The Ring Bearers

One or two boys chosen to carry the rings down the aisle to the best man.

The Groomsmen and Ushers

The groomsmen help the best man, and the ushers show the wedding guests to their seats at the wedding ceremony.

Your Part in the Wedding

Some brides have only one bridesmaid and one flower girl, but others choose a small group of friends and relatives. If you're a flower girl, you will carry flowers or a small basket containing flower petals, which—if the rules of the ceremony site permit—you will scatter in the bride's path as she walks down the aisle. After the ceremony, you will follow the couple up the aisle. If you're a junior bridesmaid, you will walk in with the other attendants, and stand with them during the ceremony.

If you have any questions about what to do on the wedding day, just ask the maid or matron of honor, or one of the other bridesmaids.

The day of the wedding is long and busy. Most ceremonies take place in the morning, but there are also afternoon and evening weddings. The following outline will give you an idea of what to expect for a morning wedding:

In the Morning

You might be asked to arrive at the bride's house early in the morning so that you can get dressed up and have your hair done. Sometimes, photographs are taken of everyone getting ready and looking pretty in their dresses before they leave for the ceremony.

The wedding ceremony might be held in a church, a courthouse, a synagogue, or some other special place. Usually there will be a short trip there from the bride's home. You might ride in a special car called a limousine with the other members of the wedding party. You will be expected to arrive at least thirty minutes before the ceremony begins. When you get there, a photographer might take more pictures of you with the bride and her other attendants.

❧11❧

During the Ceremony

Once the bride arrives, the bridesmaids should help to straighten out her dress, veil, and train.

When the music starts, the bridesmaids and groomsmen begin to walk slowly down the aisle in pairs. The flower girl and the ring bearer go next, often together. If it is allowed, the flower girl may scatter flower petals from a basket. Finally, the bride and her father walk down the aisle together.

In a church, the priest or minister usually stands facing the bride and groom at the altar steps. In a synagogue, the couple is married by a rabbi under a *chuppah*, or wedding canopy. In a courthouse, the couple stands before a judge or clerk of the court during the ceremony.

The wedding party usually remains standing for most of the ceremony, although you may be asked to sit at certain times. At the end of the ceremony, the entire wedding party follows the bride and groom as they leave.

More photographs will then be taken before the bride and groom are showered with birdseed, rice, flower petals, or confetti. Then they leave for the reception, usually in a limousine.

The Reception

After another short car ride, the bridesmaids arrive at the reception, just after the bride and groom. You may be asked to stand in the receiving line. This is the bride and groom's chance to greet all the guests personally.

At a formal reception, the guests will be served a full meal. If the reception is less formal, there might be a buffet where the guests can serve themselves. When everyone has eaten, the bride's father and the best man will give little speeches called toasts to wish the bride and groom happiness in their life together. Then the wedding cake is cut and served to the guests.

At some weddings, there will be dancing before the bride and groom leave.

The Send-off

Everyone will want to see the bride and groom leave in style. All the guests cheer, and they may throw rice or confetti at the couple. Just before they go, the bride will throw her bouquet to her female guests. It is said that the one who catches it will be the next person to get married!

Here is space to write how you feel about being asked to be in the wedding.

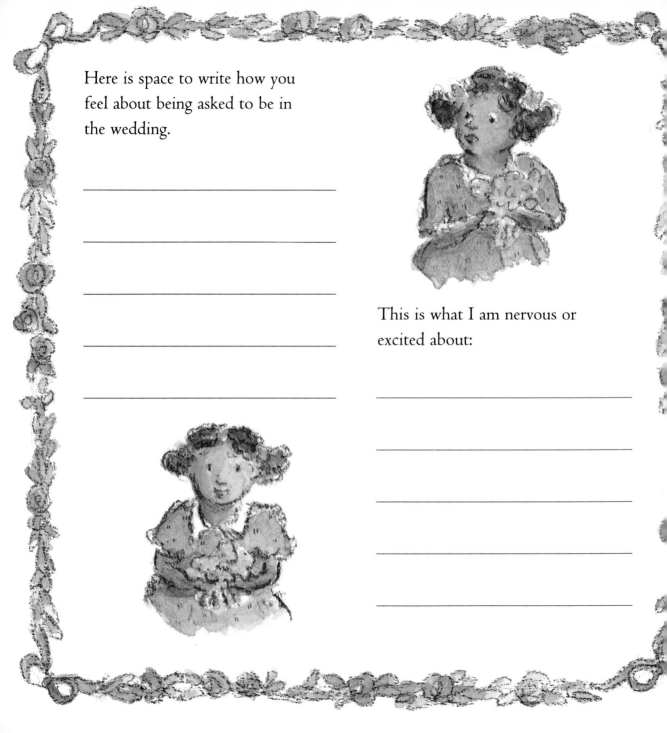

_____

_____

_____

_____

_____

This is what I am nervous or excited about:

_____

_____

_____

_____

_____

Things to Practice

There will be a stretch of time during the ceremony when you will have to sit still and be patient, so be prepared to just enjoy the quiet parts. But also be ready to dance with the guests and cheer for the bride and groom at the reception!

Since you will have your picture taken over and over again, you might also want to practice your best smiles in the mirror.

Practice walking very slowly up and down a long hallway so that you get a feeling for your walk down the aisle on the day of the wedding.

Photo & Drawing Section

On their wedding day, the bride and groom will be wearing special clothes and will look different than they usually do. Take a photograph of them, or draw a picture, showing what they look like on a normal day in their ordinary clothes.

Clothes and Shoes

One of the best things about being in a wedding party is that you will be given a pretty dress and special shoes to wear. Your dress might be made of silk, velvet, tulle, or cotton, and it will probably be in one of the bride's favorite colors. Your dress might match the other bridesmaids' dresses, or each dress might be different.

Either you will go to a dressmaker to be measured and fitted for your dress, or you will go on a special shopping trip to buy one. There are many stores that sell only dresses for brides and their attendants.

You will probably need to buy some special shoes, too. They might be shiny satin slippers dyed to match your dress, patent-leather shoes, or sandals. Be sure to tell someone right away if your dress or your shoes seem too tight or uncomfortable.

My dress is made of

_____

The color of my dress is

_____

My dress is being made by

_____

The date of my first fitting is

_____

The date of my final fitting is

_____

My dress was bought from

_____

The color of my shoes is

_____

My shoes are made out of

_____

My shoes were bought from

_____

Things to Practice

Walking in a pair of jeans and sneakers is quite different from walking in a special dress and shoes. Your dress will probably be longer and fuller than any you have worn before. It would be a good idea to practice walking in your dress before the wedding. If you have the dress at home, be very careful when you try it on—you wouldn't want to risk ripping it or accidentally spilling something on it.

It is also important to make sure that you can walk in your new shoes without slipping or tripping. Try walking around in them, but don't wear them outside. You want them to look brand-new on the day of the wedding—not scuffed and dirty. If the soles of your shoes are slippery, ask someone to buy you some nonslip adhesive treads to put on the bottoms. And don't forget to take the price tag off the soles!

Because you will be riding in a car in your pretty new clothes and shoes, practice sitting down and standing up without wrinkling your dress. The place where the ceremony is to be held might have steps leading to the door, so you will also want to try going up and down stairs without catching your shoes in the hem of your dress. You wouldn't want to trip or fall! Finally, if you can, find a good place to tuck a tissue or handkerchief in case your nose runs during the ceremony.

Photo & Drawing Section

Draw your dress and shoes here. You could ask someone to take a picture of you while you are being fitted for your dress, and then put the photograph here.

Hair

You might be asked to go to a hair salon to find out what kind of hairstyle you should have on the wedding day. The style will depend on the length of your hair and the type of headpiece that you will wear. If you wear a headpiece, it might be a hat, a headband, or a small garland of real or artificial flowers that match your dress. The hairdresser might practice a few different styles to make sure your headpiece stays in place and your hair doesn't fall in your eyes. Bobby pins or barrettes and hair spray might help to hold your hair in place.

On the wedding day, your special hairdo might be styled by a hairdresser, another member of the wedding party, or a relative.

The hairdresser's name is

_____

I went to the hairdresser for
the first time on

_____

The color of my headpiece is

_____

My headpiece is made of

_____

Things to Practice

On the day of the wedding, you will need to be careful that your hair doesn't get tousled. Ask if you can practice wearing your headpiece for a little while so that you get used to it. It will probably be fairly fragile, though, so don't play any rough games in it. Make sure that you practice walking with your chin up so that the wedding guests are able to see your face. You might also want to practice getting in and out of the car with your dress and headpiece. You'll need to duck as you get into the car so that you don't catch your headpiece on the doorframe. And if you have a long dress, don't forget to lift it carefully, making sure it is inside the car before the door is closed.

Photo & Drawing Section

Ask someone to take a picture of you with your hair done, or draw a picture of your headpiece here:

Others in the Wedding Party

You may already know all or some of the bride's other attendants. They could be your sisters or cousins, or friends of the bride and groom. The maid or matron of honor makes sure that everyone knows what to do on the wedding day.

A short while before the wedding, the bride will arrange for you to meet the other members of the wedding party. This might be when you have the first fitting for your special clothes, or you might meet at a party arranged so you can all get to know one another. (Don't forget to make a note of who they all are in the record section on the following pages.)

Other Attendants

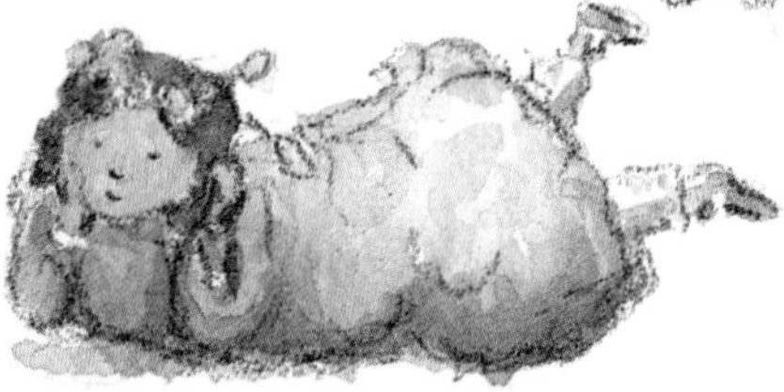

1 _____

She knows the bride and groom
because

_____

2 _____

She knows the bride and groom
because

_____

3 _____

She knows the bride and groom
because

_____

4 _____

She knows the bride and groom
because

_____

5 _____

She knows the bride and groom
because

_____

6 _____

She knows the bride and groom
because

_____

Other Attendants

4 _____

He knows the bride and groom
because

_____

1 _____

He knows the bride and groom
because

_____

5 _____

He knows the bride and groom
because

_____

2 _____

He knows the bride and groom
because

_____

6 _____

He knows the bride and groom
because

_____

3 _____

He knows the bride and groom
because

_____

Things to Practice

It is very important that you get along with all the other people in the wedding party, so if you don't already know them, do try to be friendly. One of the reasons the bride and groom have asked you to be in their wedding is because they know that you will do a great job.

Remember who comes before and after you in the procession. Just as an actor has a cue to come on stage or say a line, there will very likely be a place in the music that you need to listen for to start marching down the aisle.

Photo & Drawing Section

Ask someone to take a photograph of you with all the others when you first get together. Or maybe you would rather draw your own picture of what everyone looks like.

The Rehearsal

ecause a wedding is a special event involving many people, there is almost always a rehearsal. This is usually held the day before the wedding and is often followed by a dinner. If you haven't met everyone in the wedding yet, this is your chance! The whole wedding party will be there, along with the bride's and groom's parents and the person who will be conducting the ceremony. The reason for the rehearsal is for all those involved to learn exactly what they will do during the ceremony and where they should walk and stand. Someone will make sure that you know exactly what to do, so don't be nervous.

The rehearsal was held on

_____

_____

It took place at

_____

_____

The people at the rehearsal were

_____

_____

_____

The rehearsal dinner was held at

_____

Things to Practice

If you've practiced everything else so far, you will be an expert at the rehearsal. Make sure that you learn where to stand and walk—if you aren't sure, ask the maid or matron of honor. Practice walking with your head up and looking straight ahead. As an added challenge, practice balancing a book on your head. That way you'll know you're keeping your head up. If you are carrying a bouquet, hold your flowers in such a way that everyone can see your face.

And don't forget to smile as much as possible throughout the day. Practice that smile!

Photo & Drawing Section

If someone takes pictures at the rehearsal, ask them to let you have a photograph to put here. Just like you, the bride will be wearing casual clothes rather than her beautiful dress, although she might wear her veil or train so she can get used to the way it feels. Draw a picture of her with the groom so you can remember how they looked.

The Wedding Day

The big day is here at last! Like everyone else involved with the wedding, you'll be very excited. Here is a countdown of things you don't want to forget.

Breakfast

Make sure you have something to eat in the morning. Food helps calm the nervous "butterflies" in your stomach. And if you've eaten breakfast, your stomach won't growl loudly during the quiet parts of the ceremony!

A Bath

You want to look and smell your best for the wedding, so take a bath or shower just after you get up in the morning. Check to see if you should wash your hair, too, or if the hairdresser will want to do this. It is important that you take your bath *before* you have your hair done so that it doesn't get wet and droopy.

Your Hair

Even though you will be impatient to get to the wedding, try to sit still while you have your hair done. If you have to visit the hairdresser at a salon, don't forget to take your headpiece. If the day is cloudy, take along an umbrella so that your hair is protected from the rain when you walk from the salon to the car.

Getting Dressed

Make sure you go to the bathroom before you get dressed. Put your tights or socks on first, because it is more difficult to get them on once you are wearing everything else. You might need to ask for help as you step into your dress and pull it up to your shoulders. (If you pull your dress on over your head, it might muss up your hair or ruin your headpiece.) Put your shoes on last.

Getting to the Ceremony

If you are given your flowers or a flower basket just before you leave for the ceremony, don't forget to take them with you! If you get carsick easily, ask if you can sit in the front seat with the window slightly open.

The Ceremony

When you get to the place where the ceremony will be held, smooth out your dress. If you need to blow your nose or go to the bathroom, do it now. Wait quietly for the bride to arrive—and don't forget to smile and say hello to her when she comes. It would be nice if you told her how beautiful she looks. Try to sit still during the ceremony and just *enjoy* being a part of it all!

The Photographs

Most of the pictures will probably be taken after the ceremony. This usually takes a while. The photographer will tell you what to do and when to do it. Don't forget to smile—no funny faces!

The Reception

If you have to go to the bathroom again when you get to the reception, don't be embarrassed to ask for help with your special clothes. After you have washed your hands, smooth out your dress again before you go back into the reception.

Every reception is different. Some include formal sit-down dinners. Some are more casual, with a buffet where the guests help themselves. Or there might be waiters and waitresses who bring the food and wine around the room to the guests. If there is a formal dinner, you might be seated at the head table, since you are part of the bridal party.

Even if you do not know the people sitting next to you very well, be sure to talk to them.

After everyone has eaten, the bride and groom cut the wedding cake. Then the best man makes a special toast to the couple with wine or champagne. Other people might make speeches, too. They can be very funny, and are always full of good wishes.

The Send-off

Eventually the bride and groom will leave the reception to go on a special trip called a honeymoon. Everyone will cheer and wish them well as they leave. Sometimes people throw more confetti, rice, birdseed, or flower petals. Be sure you have some to throw, too. Just before the bride leaves, she turns her back to her female guests and tosses her bouquet over her shoulder. See if you can catch it! (Turn back to page 15 if you can't remember why.) Take a little piece of wedding cake home with you. Wrap it in a napkin or a plastic bag and put it under your pillow before you go to sleep. To find out why, turn to page 61.

There were _____ people at the wedding. Here are the names of the people I met there:

_____   _____   _____

_____   _____   _____

_____   _____

_____   _____

_____   _____

_____   _____

_____   _____   _____

_____   _____   _____

The weather was

_____

I thought that the wedding
ceremony was

_____

The reception was held at

_____

This is what we had to eat and drink

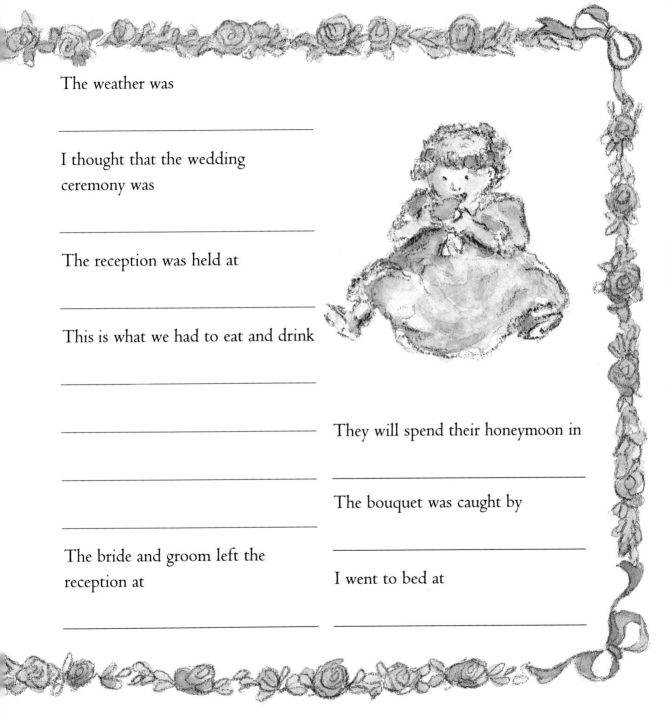

_____

_____

They will spend their honeymoon in

_____

The bouquet was caught by

_____

The bride and groom left the
reception at

I went to bed at

_____

_____

You can press some of your flowers or flower petals and keep them here. To do this, put them between two sheets of waxed paper inside a heavy book. You could make a special picture with them and decorate it with confetti or birdseed. When the wedding photographs are developed, you will probably be given one, so you could keep it here to remind you of how nice you all looked at the wedding.

There is also a special envelope in the front of this book where you can keep your wedding souvenirs, such as the invitation, the ceremony program, and any other wedding things.

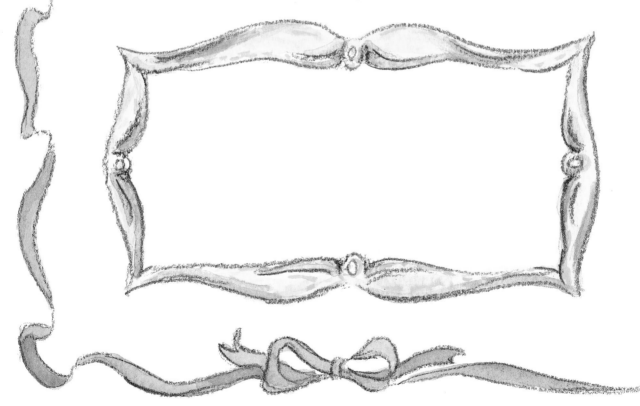

The Day After the Wedding

After the wedding, you might be feeling a little sad that all the excitement is over. This would be a good time to finish writing your records and memories of the day. Remembering all the happy things will cheer you up.

You should write to the bride and her parents to thank them for including you in such a special day. If the groom gave you a present, you should also write to him.

Here are some ideas about what you could write in your thank-you notes:

To the Bride

Dear

'Thank you for asking me to be a bridesmaid at your wedding. I had a lovely time and felt very special in my pretty clothes. I thought that you looked beautiful.

With love from,

To the Groom

Dear

'Thank you for your special gift which I will always treasure. I thought you made a handsome groom and I really enjoyed my day as a bridesmaid.

With love from,

To the Bride's Parents

Dear

'Thank you for the lovely wedding reception. I really enjoyed it and thought the food was scrumptious. The bride looked beautiful.

With love from,

The Wedding Cake

There is a legend that says that if you go to sleep with a piece of wedding cake under your pillow, you will have sweet dreams of the man you are going to marry! Did you remember to save some of the cake?

The things I liked best about being in the wedding were

_____

_____

_____

_____

_____